10 Steps
To Writing
A Best Seller Book

Giovanni Dangel

Table of Contents

Introduction

I want to thank you and congratulate you for downloading the book, *"10 steps to writing a best seller Book"*

This book was specifically written for people interested in learning how to publish on kindle or for people who have already published on kindle and want to sell more books.

There was a time when writing a book was a dream that was hard to achieve. In this modern day, with the internet so readily available, book writing is becoming a very common activity.

Whether you are doing it to fulfill your dream, or if you are breaking into the writing industry for your job, there are still things you need to know for your book.

You can erase the idea that you are going to sit down and write the book start to finish right now. This is a lengthy process that takes time, effort, but most of all, research.

This book will show you how to come up with an idea for your book, help you format it properly for Kindle, assist you in writing it, and show you how to publish it. Finally, you will learn how to market you book into bestseller status.

Thanks again for downloading this book, I hope you enjoy it!

Are you ready to transform your life and reach your optimal potential?

VISIT:

Step 1
Book Topics

Whether this is your first book or your 20th book, you need an idea. The best place to start is to look at your interests, hobbies, and skills. What are you good at? What is your job? What are your hobbies? If you pick a topic you know a lot about, your book will be easy to write, especially if it is a topic you are passionate about.

Try making a list of your hobbies, interests, and skills. The next step is to do some online research to see if any of your listed book topics have the potential to be bestsellers.

Step 2
Research

Now that you have a list of your interests, skills, and hobbies, you can start some online research to see if there is a market for any of your listed items. The research is easy. Simply go to Amazon.com and see what is out there for sale and if it is selling. Follow these steps to do that:

Go to www.amazon.com
Click on "Books & Audible" on the left, which will open up a new list beside it, then click on "Kindle Books" (see picture below)

amazon
Try Prime   Barbara's Amazon.com   Today's Deals   Gift Cards

Shop by
Department ⌄   Search   All ⌄

Unlimited Instant Videos	Books
MP3s & Cloud Player	Books
20 million songs, play anywhere	Kindle Books
Amazon Cloud Drive	Children's Books
5 GB of free storage	
Kindle Books & E-readers	Textbooks
Kindle Fire Tablets	Magazines
Appstore for Android	
Get eWallet for free today	Sell Your Books
Digital Games & Software	
	Audible Audiobooks
Books & Audible >	Audible Membership
Movies, Music & Games	Get to know Audible
Electronics & Computers	Audible Audiobooks & More
Home, Garden & Tools	Whispersync for Voice
Beauty, Health & Grocery	Switch between reading and listening

Now click on "Kindle Bestsellers" on the left (see picture below)

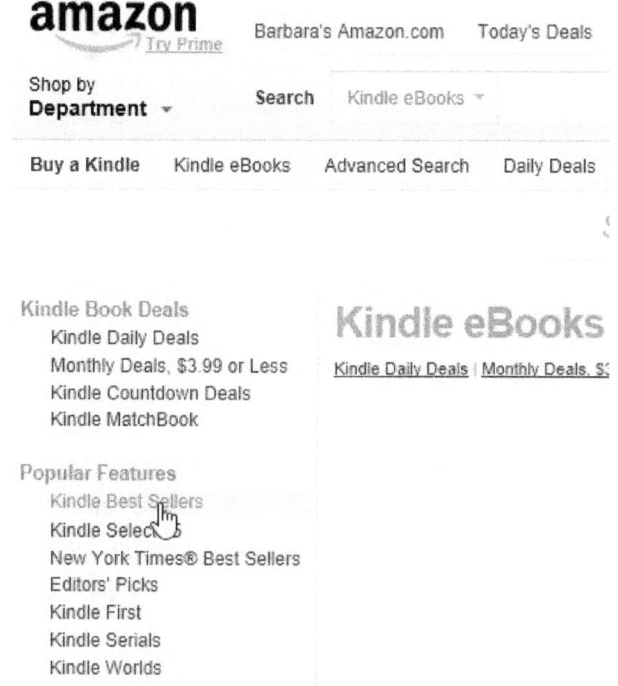

You will notice a list of subject categories on the left. On the right will be the 100 Bestsellers in each category that you click on. The picture below shows the categories. Note that once you click on a specific category, other sub-categories will become available to search (for example, if you click on "Cookbooks, Food, and Wine" a lot of other categories will open up such as Baking, Canning, Drinks & Beverages)

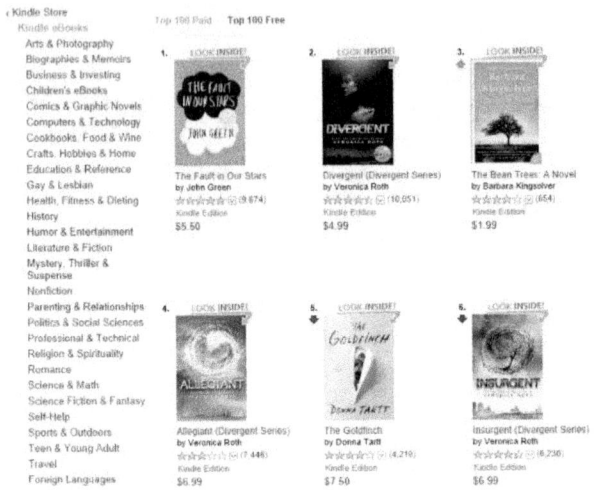

The next step is to find the categories that best suit your areas of interest, hobbies, and skills. Take a look at the bestselling books in those categories. See if you can come up with an idea for a book that you could write. For example, if you look in the Baking category and see that there are a lot of cookie recipe books in the top 100 bestsellers, perhaps you could write a cookbook on cookies (if that is one of your interests).

The idea is to find a potential book topic that is currently selling on the bestsellers list and that is also one of your identified topics. By choosing a topic that you are interested in, your book will be easy and fun for you to write.

Step 3
Book Title and Outline

Looking at the bestsellers in your categories should give you an idea of what is selling. Try clicking on each bestseller that is in your area of interest, or **niche market**. Look at that book's title and subtitle. Try to come up with a title and subtitle for your book. Of course, you do not want to copy the title and subtitle of any book that already exists on amazon, but you may see words or phrases that are common to many books. For example, many of the cookie cookbooks might say "quick and easy recipes" or "delicious cookie recipes". If many of the bestsellers in your category use those phrases in the title or subtitle, consider adding them to your title or subtitle as well.

Next, you want to think about the content of your book. You don't want to actually write it at this time, but you want to start with an outline. What will the chapter titles of your book consist of? What will the headings and sub-headings in each chapter consist of?

A good place to start is to (again!) look at the bestselling books in your topic. You can usually see the contents of a book by clicking on the book cover on its listing page. There is usually a "Look Inside" feature that allows you to see the first 5-10% of a particular book. You can get an idea of what chapter titles and headings are in those books. That will give you an idea of what you want and don't want inside your book.

Now that you have idea of what your book is about, the title and subtitle for your book, and an idea of the contents of your book, it is time to start writing and formatting your new book!

Step 4
How to Format Your Book

Word

The formatting section of this book is written for Word 2010, however, all of the features are also available in Word 2007, 2013, and even 2003. Whichever version you are using, simple search for the topic in the tabs or menus of the version you are using. If you cannot find a certain feature, I would suggest you visit your favorite search engine and type in something like, "how to do * in Word 2011", replacing the * with the feature you are looking for and replacing 2011 with the version you currently are working in. This is what I do for my books and with my college students and we have had great success finding the answers we are looking for.

Formatting

This section contains details on how to format each part of your new Kindle book. I know that a lot of people find formatting to be intimidating and frustrating. Please don't feel this way. Always remember that anything you do can be undone. It is never written in stone.
Have fun!

Page Size

Let's start with the page size of your manuscript. The majority of books are either 8.5" x 11" or 6" x 9". Once you upload your book to be published, it will be converted to a file format that will be compatible with all electronic devices.

In order to choose or change your page size, go to the Page Layout tab and in the Page Setup group, drop down the arrow under the option Size. Choose the size you want.

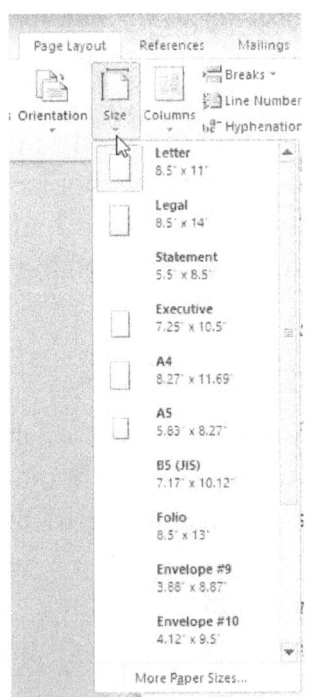

If the size you want is not listed, click on More
Paper Sizes and manually enter the height and
width of your page.

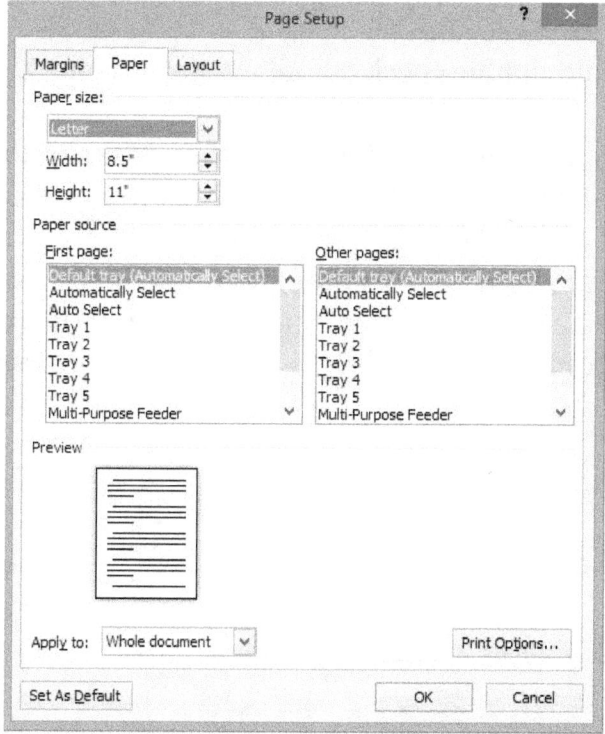

Margins

Next, let's set the margins of your manuscript. Your computer may be set with proper margins, but every computer setting is different, so we should double check before we start writing.

To check the margins of your document, go to the Page Layout tab, in the Page Setup group, and click on the arrow below the option, Margins. A good option for Kindle books is the Normal option, which is a 1" margin on the top, bottom, right, and left. If it is not already selected, choose Normal.

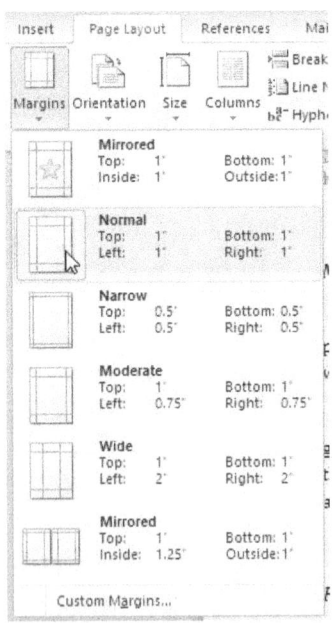

Paragraph Settings

Now, let's take a look at your paragraph settings.

The elements of paragraph settings that we are concerned with are line spacing and the space before and after your headings (we will learn about headings in the next section).

I will explain these settings here and then we will see how they are affected in the Styles section below.

To see the default paragraph settings for your Word document, go to the Home tab in the Paragraph group. You will see an icon that looks like lines of text with blue arrows pointing up and down. Click on the down arrow on that icon.

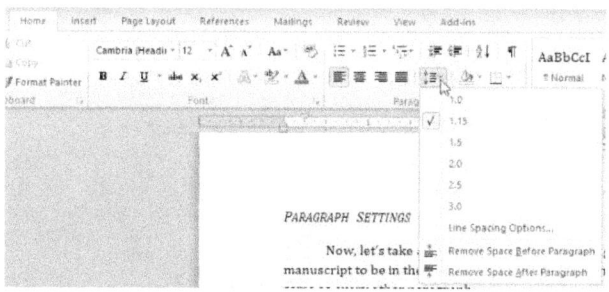

You will see that the example above shows a line spacing of 1.15 (slightly more than single-spaced). Both options at the bottom say Remove

Space Before/After Paragraph. The other option here is that one or both of these options could say Add Space Before/After Paragraph. Right now, the program is adding space both before a new paragraph and after a paragraph. These extra spaces make the paragraphs and sections of your book easier to read. If I wanted to remove these spaces, I could click on the word Remove and then the next time I dropped down this menu, it would say Add.

Note that if you want to change the setting that is on your computer, you first need to select your entire text and then make the change. You can select your entire text by going to the Home tab and clicking on the arrow beside Select in the Editing group. Then, choose Select All.

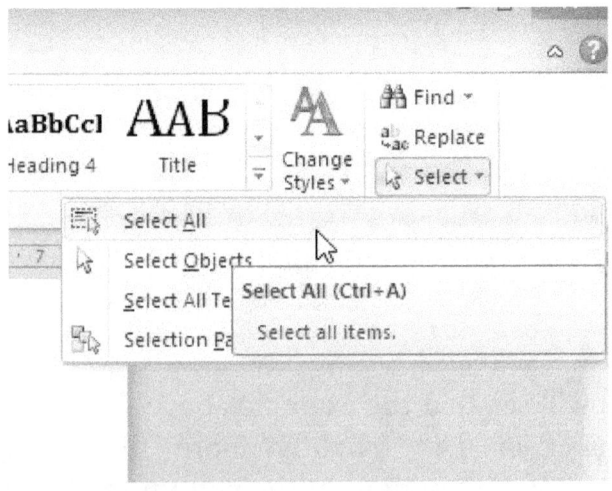

If you would like to have each paragraph indented on the first line, take these steps:

- Select the text in your manuscript
- Right-click and choose Paragraph
- Ensure that the Indents and Spacing tab is selected
- Under Indentation, Special, click on the drop-down arrow and choose First line
- Click OK

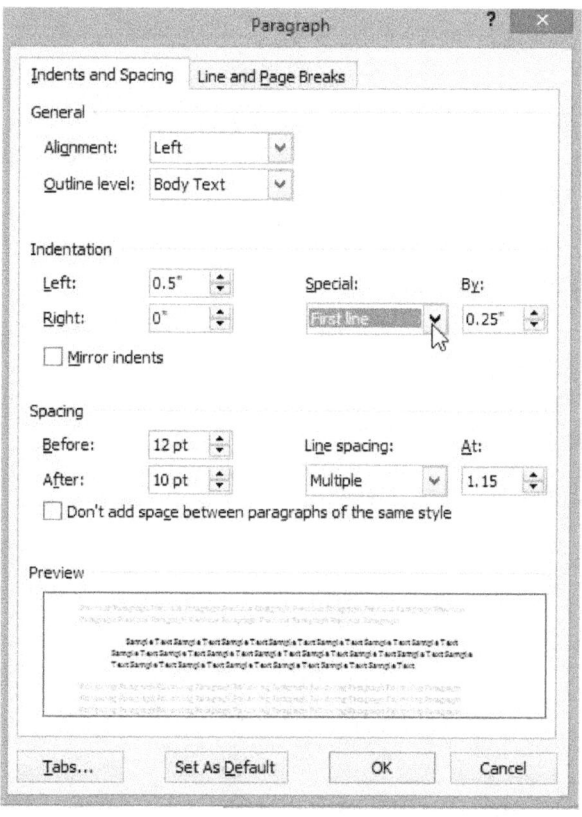

Headings

In the Home tab, in the Styles group, you will notice a number of pre-set Styles. You can drop down the arrow at the far right of that group to see quite a few more.

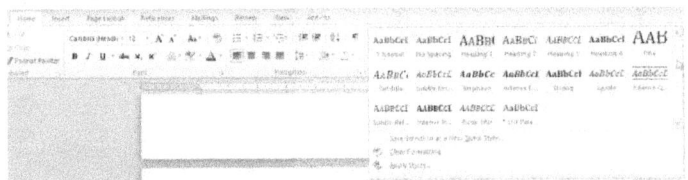

For your manuscript, we will be looking at the Title, Subtitle, Heading 1, Heading 2, Heading 3, and Normal Styles.

Let's start by actually typing out part of your book. You are about to start writing now – congratulations!

Styles and Themes

It is a good idea to choose a Style for your manuscript. By choosing a Style, your manuscript will have a consistent look and feel about it, your headings will all be formatted the same, and your Table of Contents will generate with just a simple mouse-click.

The default Style is seen in the example above. You may prefer something different, or you may prefer this Style, but in a different color scheme. Both are possible.

Before you choose a Style, place your mouse at a position in your manuscript where you can see a couple of headings and some text. That way, when you peruse the Styles, you will see automatically what they will look like before you choose one.

To choose a Style, go to the Home tab, in the Styles group (group names are written under each section in the ribbon at the top of your screen). Drop down the arrow beside Change Styles and move your mouse to Style Set. A list of pre-set Styles will become available to you.

As you place your mouse on each of the options, the text on your screen will take on the attributes of that Style, showing you what your manuscript would look like if you choose that one. Choose one that you like.

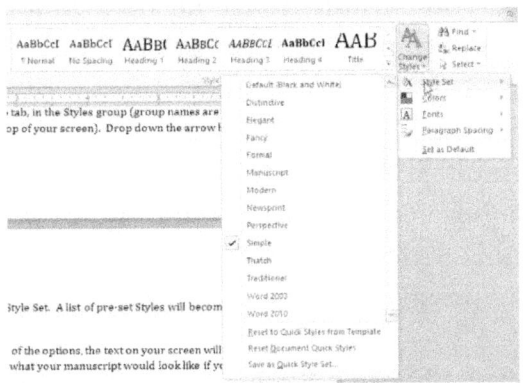

size will be chosen for you as well. You will see that the Heading 1, Heading 2, and Heading 3 Styles that show in the Home tab are now the same as the ones you chose in your selected Style.

It is very important that your entire manuscript follow the same Style throughout. Specifically, the font of your paragraphs should all be the same font type and size. If you chose a Style where the paragraph font is Cambria 12pt, then all of the paragraph text in your entire manuscript should be Cambria 12pt (like this one). In this way, you will be able to deliver a professionally formatted manuscript that looks great on any device.

Color Schemes

Once you have chosen a Style that you like, you may wish to change the color scheme. You can do this by going to the Home tab, in the Styles group and clicking on the arrow beside the Change Styles option. Put your mouse on the Colors option and all of the pre-set color schemes will now be available to you. As you move your cursor over each color scheme, your manuscript will show how the Title, Subtitle, and Heading Styles look when that color scheme is applied. Choose one that you like.

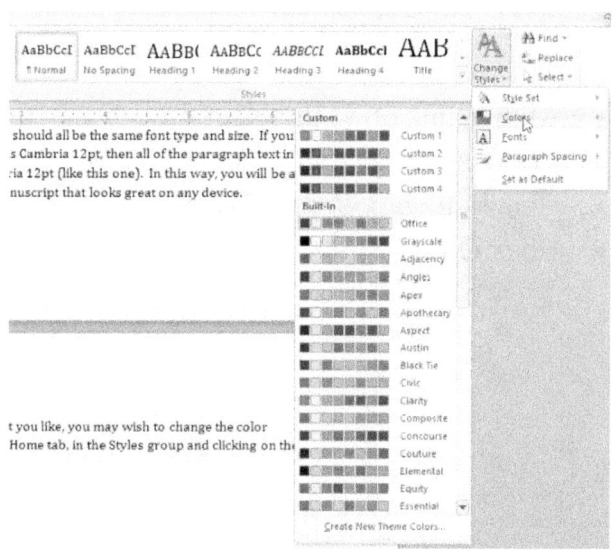

Keep With Next

As you begin writing your book, you will have a lot of headings and subheadings followed by the text of your book. Wherever possible, you should have the paragraph heading and the text that follows it on the same page. If that is not possible, there should be at least 2 lines of text following each paragraph heading. If a heading ends up at the bottom of a page all by itself, it looks unprofessional. To prevent this from happening, do the following:

Select your paragraph heading and the first two lines of text that follow it

- Right-click on your selection
- Choose Paragraph
- Check the box Keep With Next
- Click OK

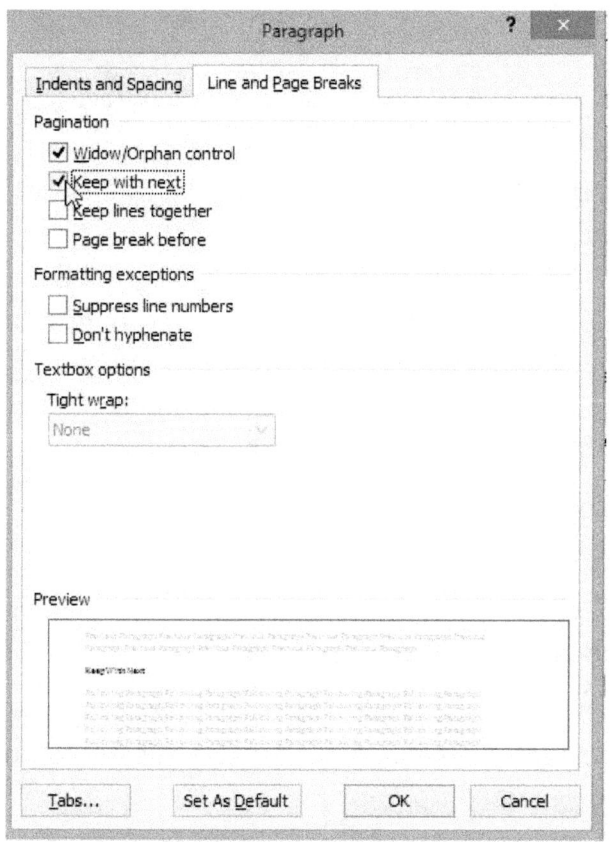

Step 5
Fixing Existing Problems

You may find yourself in one of the following situations:

- You have a book that has previously been published on Amazon Kindle and you have received some negative reviews referring to formatting

- You have published a book but want to fix the formatting

- You have outsourced a book and need to fix the formatting

- You wrote a book, but were not sure how to correctly format it and now certain features are messed up

- I have known many authors in one of these situations who resorted to re-typing their manuscript from scratch in order to fix a formatting issue that they couldn't resolve on their own. If you find yourself in a similar circumstance, you don't have to re-type your book. You can actually remove all of the existing formatting and just be left with the text.

Step 6 Proofread

Now that you have finished writing your book, it must be edited and proofread. You can never proofread too much. It can be very hard to see all of the spelling and grammatical errors in a manuscript while looking at it on the computer screen. Here are some tips for finding all the errors in your book, so that they can be fixed:

Take a break – step away from your manuscript. Go have lunch, take a walk, work on something else, or get some exercise. The break will allow you to have fresh eyes when you look at it again. You may catch errors that you didn't notice the first time around

Print your manuscript – you may not like this option as it will use more paper and ink and is less environmentally friendly. However, it will allow you to see more mistakes on paper than you would see on the computer screen

Try reading your book out loud. You may feel silly doing this; however, forcing yourself to read the words will allow you to see more errors than just skimming over them. When you skim over them without reading them out loud, your brain sees what it wants to see, instead of what is actually there

Step 7 Amazon KDP Account

You have now finished writing and formatting your book. Congratulations on a job well done!

At this point, you need to make sure you are completely happy with your book. Also, you should have received your cover back from Fiverr. If you have both of those items ready, you can move on to publishing.

Now, you need to publish your book on Amazon's Kindle platform, Kindle Direct Publishing. Here is the link to sign up:

http://kdp.amazon.com

Once you have created your KDP account, you will gain access to the KDP dashboard, which looks like this:

KDP Select

The first section explains about the KDP Select program and asks if you want to enroll your book in this program. Take a minute to read about it. It allows Amazon Prime members to borrow your book for free. That is, it is free for them. You receive part of the KDP Select Global Fund Amount, which is usually about $1.2 million per month. Amazon takes all of the borrows and divides up the $1.2 million between the publishers of those books. Your enrollment only lasts 90 days and you can opt-out after any 90 day period.

Be sure to read all of the restrictions associated with this program. You are not allowed to sell your book on other sales sites not associated with Amazon, but in return, you get to promote your book to Amazon's users for a total of 5 free days in each 90 day enrollment period. We will discuss more about how to promote your book in the next chapter on marketing.

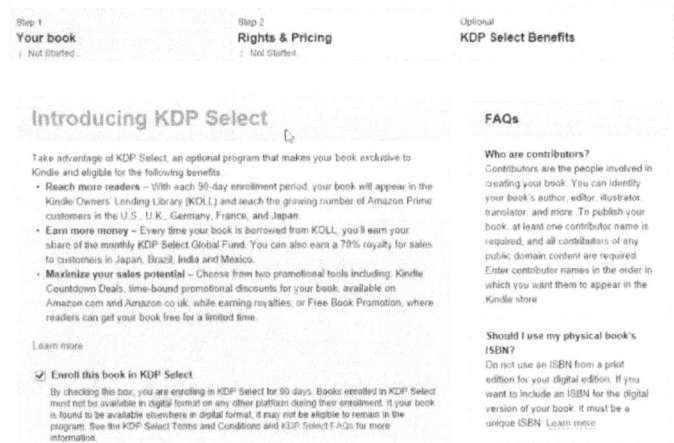

Book Name

Add the title of your book in this section. Be sure you spell everything properly and using capital letters wherever necessary.

Subtitle

Add the subtitle of your book in this section. Be sure you spell everything properly and using capital letters wherever necessary. Indicate if your book is part of a series and the edition number.

Publisher

If you have a company, put the company name as the publisher. Otherwise, you may add your name as the publisher.

Description

Write a compelling description of your book that will entice people to buy it.

Book Contributors

Here, you will add all of the contributors to your book. You may be the only author, or you may have shared the writing with someone else or other people. If you are writing a children's book, you may want to add the illustrator as a contributor. Click on Add Contributor and fill in the screen that follows for each contributor.

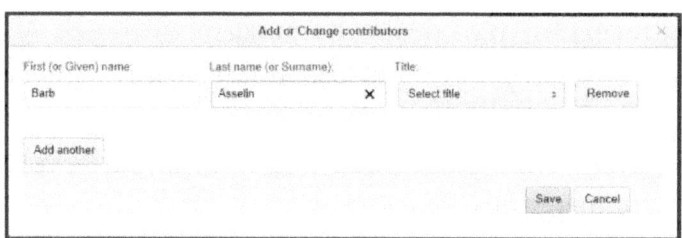

Step 8 Graphics

You may want to add graphics to your manuscript. If you do, keep the following things in mind:

- Each graphic should be centered on your page, like the graphics in this book
- There should never be an text beside your graphic
- Once you add a graphic, you will see a new tab at the top of your ribbon, called Picture Tools. This tab can be used to add a border to your graphics, align them, or crop them
- When you sell a book on Amazon, Amazon charges a "delivery fee". The more graphics you have in your book, the higher your delivery fee will be. Always re-size your graphics in a graphics program such as Paint so that they are the correct size when you insert them into your manuscript
- To add a graphic to your manuscript, you can do it one of two ways:
- Copy the graphic and paste it into your manuscript in the correct spot, or
- Go to the Insert tab and choose Picture from the Illustrations group. Browse to find your picture and click Insert

Step 9 How to Market Your Book

Now that you have published your book, it is time to start selling it! These are the steps to get your books on the Kindle bestsellers' lists.

KDP Select Benefits Section

The KDP dashboard offers you two ways to promote your book, as long as your book is enrolled in the KDP Select Benefits promotion.

Free Book Promotion

For every 90 day enrollment period, you get five free days to promote your new book. That means that you can offer your book for free to anyone to download for five days. You don't need to use all five days at once, and often it would be much better if you didn't. You can use one day at a time, or two days at once, or any combination that adds up to five days over a 90 day period.

You may be wondering why you would want to offer your book for free. How can you make money that way? Well, two things can get your book to bestseller status. The first is sales. In order to get sales, people need to want to buy your book. The second is reviews. Amazon readers are likely to read the reviews of a book before they purchase it.

By offering your book for free, you are giving people a chance to download you book without paying for it. The more people that download your book, there is a greater likelihood that some of them will leave you some reviews. Since you did a fantastic job writing and formatting your book and you chose a topic that you are passionate and knowledgeable about, the reviews should be great.

Kindle Countdown Deal

KDP also offers you the Kindle Countdown Deal to promote your book. For every 90 day promotion period, you can run Kindle Countdown Deals that reduce your book's price for a set period of time. For example, your book may regularly sell at $2.99. During a Kindle Countdown Deal, you can offer your book for $0.99 for 1 week and then $1.99 for 1 week, and then the price goes back to $2.99 after two weeks. This creates urgency in your book and may generate more sales.

The only stipulation is that you cannot do both the Free Book Promotion and the Kindle Countdown Deal in the same 90 day period. You must choose one.

Borrows

As part of the KDP Select option, your book can also be downloaded for free by anyone in the Kindle Unlimited program (KU). If this happens, you don't get any money for the sale of the book, however, you do get a certain amount of money per page read, which is referred to in "kindle language" as KENP. The amount started out at half a cent per page. It has gone down some, however, some money is better than no money and if you have a 300 page book and someone reads all of it, you may end up with more money than you would have had if someone bought it.

Social Media

If you have social media accounts, you can use them to promote your Kindle books as well.

Twitter

On Twitter, there are a few ways you can promote your books:

You can post a link to your book when you publish it

You can post a link to your book when you run your free promotions or kindle countdown promotions

You can "follow" other writers and publishers or people with the same interests as you and hope that they follow you back

You can tweet your book with the following hashtags to encourage people with Amazon Prime accounts to borrow your books: #borrow #amazon prime

Facebook

On Facebook, there are many ways you can promote your books as well:

You can post a link to your book when you publish it

You can post a link to your book when you run your free promotions or kindle countdown promotions

You can create a Facebook page for your book and ask people to "like" it

You can "join" author and publisher and kindle groups and post your free book promotions on those groups

Step 10 Marketing Action Plan

I have created a marketing plan for you. Feel free to follow it, or amend it to suit your needs.

Day of Launch

Test to make sure all links work and that it looks good when downloaded on a device.

Set up promotions in KDP dashboard.

1 day this week
2 days, 5 weeks later
2 days, 5 or 6 weeks later (for a total of 5 days, spread out over the 90 day period)

Give yourself reminder on each of these days to promote your book

Give yourself reminder at end of 90-day period to set up new promotions

Add your book to your Author Central Account.

Join as many Facebook groups relating to authors, kindle books, and publishing as you can.

Each Promo Day

Post a link to your book on your personal Facebook page, Twitter page, LinkedIn profile, and other social media sites that you may have accounts on.

Post a link to your book on each of the Facebook Groups that you have joined.

Goal is to get 5-10 reviews from your very first promo day so that your book is in a good position to do the next promo days.

Day after Free Promo

Post a link to your book on your personal Twitter page and include #borrow and #amazonprime and #kindleunlimited to get more borrows.

Conclusion

Thank you again for downloading this book!

Turn your previously unpublished writing projects into a published Kindle book. Market your existing manuscripts and books into Kindle bestsellers. I hope that you feel that you are now equipped with the knowledge to start and complete writing a book to be published on Amazon Kindle.

I also hope that the book your write after reading this book won't be the only book you write. The more books your write, the more money you can make. I truly believe that writing Kindle books can generate a very comfortable full-time income for anyone who loves writing or publishing and follows the steps.

Finally, if you enjoyed this book, then I'd like to ask you for a favor, would you be kind enough to leave a review for this book on Amazon? It'd be greatly appreciated!

Click here to leave a review for this book on Amazon!

Thank you and good luck!